WALKS AROUND HOLMFIRTH

TEN GREAT WALKS OF SIX MILES OR UNDER

Andrew Gallon

Dalesman

First published in 2013 by Dalesman
an imprint of
Country Publications Ltd
The Water Mill
Broughton Hall
Skipton
North Yorkshire BD23 3AG
www.dalesman.co.uk

Text © Andrew Gallon 2013
Maps © Simon Vandelt 2013
Illustrations © Christine Isherwood 2013

Cover: upper Holme Valley, by Richard Littlewood

ISBN 978-1-85568-314-3

Printed in Singapore by Tien Wah Press.

PUBLISHER'S NOTE

The information given in this book has been provided in good faith and is intended only as a general guide. Whilst all reasonable efforts have been made to ensure that details were correct at the time of publication, the author and Country Publications Ltd cannot accept any responsibility for inaccuracies. It is the responsibility of individuals undertaking outdoor activities to approach the activity with caution and, especially if inexperienced, to do so under appropriate supervision. The activity described in this book is strenuous and individuals should ensure that they are suitably fit before embarking upon it. They should carry the appropriate equipment and maps, be properly clothed and have adequate footwear. They should also take note of weather conditions and forecasts, and leave notice of their intended route and estimated time of return.

Contents

Introduction

Walks Around Last of the Summer Wine Country could be an alternative title for this book. Holmfirth, a small milltown in a quiet Pennine valley at the confluence of the rivers Holme and Ribble, is linked inextricably with the BBC situation comedy which showcased the area's glorious scenery. Its eccentric characters might have disappeared from mainstream TV, but repeats available to multi-channel viewers ensure continuing popularity for a series axed in 2010 after a run of almost forty years.

Truth is, though, even without a *Last of the Summer Wine* connection, Holmfirth and its surrounding area merit serious attention. This is a beautiful corner of Yorkshire and superb walking country. The lush, often moody, landscape typifies the Pennines, and is characterised by narrow, wooded valleys, historic riverbank settlements whose growth owed much to textile manufacture, quicksilver streams, glittering reservoirs, lofty hamlets, isolated farms, breezy moors, and mile upon mile of gritstone walls.

Our selection of walks does not stray far from Holmfirth and the dale into which it is shoehorned. Neighbouring Hepworth, Holme, Holmbridge, Netherthong and Meltham all feature as do, a little further afield, Clayton West, Denby Dale and Upper Cumberworth. We go north to Castle Hill, high above Huddersfield, south to the Dark Peak hamlet of Dunford Bridge, and west to Marsden and Slaithwaite in the Colne Valley.

Owing to the stunning scenery, the area's footpaths are well trodden. Excellent signing and waymarking ensures you are unlikely to encounter navigational problems. Whilst the sketch maps accompanying each walk should ensure trouble-free route-finding, OS maps are strongly advised, and the relevant ones are detailed in the information panel at the start of each walk.

The Holmfirth district is connected by bus to Huddersfield, Wakefield and Glossop, with feeder services linking its smaller communities. Rail branches to Holmfirth and Meltham, along with the famous Woodhead route through Dunford Bridge, are long abandoned, but Marsden retains an operational station. Clayton West and Shelley are served by the narrow-gauge Kirklees Light Railway. To help with journey planning, visit the informative websites www.yorkshiretravel.net and www.wymetro.com.

Farnley Tyas and Castle Hill

Distance: 3 miles (5km). Time: 1½-2 hours.
Start: Farnley Tyas, free street parking; grid ref 164127.
Terrain: ascents and descents, not too taxing. Height gained: 540 feet (165m).
Refreshments/facilities: pub in Farnley Tyas; no public toilets.
Public transport: Bus 341 (Huddersfield–Stocksmoor), Bus 911
(Meltham Circular).
Map: Ordnance Survey Explorer 288 Bradford & Huddersfield.

Views of Kirklees do not get better than from Castle Hill, crowned with the majestic Victoria Tower. Beginning in Farnley Tyas, a loftily located village, removes a lot of the toil which can otherwise be required to reach this iconic Pennine landmark.

Start from the Golden Cock alongside the crossroads in Farnley Tyas. With your back to the pub, turn left on Woodsome Road. Within 25 yards, drop left on a track signalled by a fingerpost. Pass through a gate and bend left to another.

Our objective, Castle Hill, is prominent across the wooded valley of Lumb Dike. This is where the outward and return routes converge.

Turn right down a steeply sloping field. A stile admits to Royd House Wood. Follow a clear path through the trees and over a stream. Swing left to emerge briefly from the wood before re-entering it. Cross another stream and eventually leave the trees via a stile.

Keep ahead along the left edge of a field and follow its boundary to the right. Climb a stile and enter Molly Carr Wood. At a junction of paths by a redundant stile, descend steps. Cross Lumb Dike on a footbridge. Climb away on steps and leave the trees via a stile. Continue along the left edge of a field. Pass through a gateway and maintain the line in the next pasture. A stile in a corner admits to Lumb Lane by dwellings known collectively as the Lumb. Turn right. Within 100 yards, leave this minor road via a stile on the left. Ascend the right edge of a steeply sloping field to a stile in a corner.

Pause to look back to Farnley Tyas, picked out by the spire of St Lucius's Church. The church dates from 1840, and was a gift of the Fourth Earl of Dartmouth, the lord of the manor.

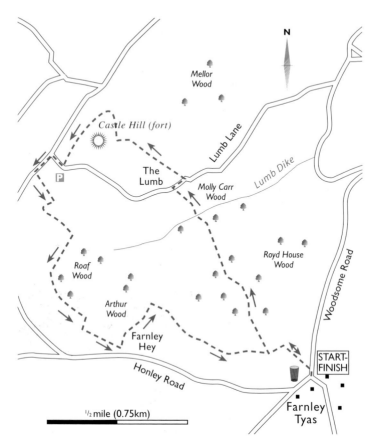

With Castle Hill and Victoria Tower looming above, continue along the right edge of the next field. Climb steps to a track. Cross it and negotiate a stile opposite. Head up the right edge of a pasture.

The towering transmitters on Emley and Holme Moss Moors become visible over to the left as height is gained.

Enter a sunken way. Climb a stile and, at a waymark post, leave the sunken way on the right. Walk along the bottom edge of a field.

Bend left. On reaching a wall, turn up to the left to a surfaced path. Bear right. Continue past an information board onto the Castle Hill plateau.

Climb steps to the right. Bear left along the edge of the plateau to Victoria Tower.

The view over Huddersfield is sensational. Castle Hill, the site of an Iron Age fort, stands at 900 feet (274m) and is a Scheduled Ancient Monument. The tower, which has 165 steps and opens regularly, was built in 1897 to mark Queen Victoria's diamond jubilee.

Keep right of the tower. Drop off Castle Hill via a flight of steps. Turn right on a minor road and then left on another at a T-junction. Within 150 yards, leave the road by a fingerpost on the left. Cross a parking area. Climb a stile into a field. Keep ahead along the field's left edge. In a corner, turn sharp right and walk across the middle of the field. Pass through a gateway at a wall corner. Turn left and head along the left edge of the adjacent field. Maintain the line over two stiles. Turn right along the top edge of a field. Climb a stile in the corner. Skirt the edge of Roaf Wood.

After a stile in a field corner, bear slightly right in the next field. Within 50 yards, turn left through a wall gap. Follow a clear path through the middle of a field. After a gap by a waymark post, continue forward in the next field. Keep left of an oak tree. Head down the side of a hedgerow to negotiate a stile and arrive in Farnley Hey.

The distinctive black-and-gold plumage of the golden plover may be spotted on the South Pennine moors in summer.

Turn left along a track, passing a row of cottages. At a dwelling called Long Meadow, bear half-right onto an enclosed way admitting to a field. Angle half-right across this and climb a stile. Turn left along the boundary of the next field and over a stile in a corner. Turn right on a track. An engraved post points to Farnley Tyas. Pass through a gate and climb a stile. Bear half-right across a sloping field. On the far side, keep right of a hedge and cross a stile in a corner. Maintain the line along the bottom edge of several fields. A final stile admits to a sloping field. Keep right of a wall and make for a gate ahead. From here, retrace your steps to Farnley Tyas.

Along the Trans-Pennine Trail

Distance: 4 miles (6.5km). **Time:** 1½-2 hours.
Start/parking: Dunford Bridge, free car park; grid ref 158023.
Terrain: gentle – former railway, field paths, steps, tracks and roads.
Height gained: 390 feet (120m).
Refreshments/facilities: none.
Public transport: Bus 25 (Holmfirth–Penistone).
Map: Ordnance Survey Explorer OL1 Peak District (Dark Peak).

Dunford Bridge is a remote hamlet in a wild landscape alongside the Upper Don river. It is at the eastern end of the triple-bore Woodhead Tunnels which, until 1981, enabled a railway between Manchester and Sheffield to burrow beneath the Pennines. The trackbed, now the Trans-Pennine Trail, is followed as far as Cote Bank Bridge before a scenic return to Dunford Bridge is made along the north flank of the valley.

Head east from the car park and follow the abandoned trackbed towards Penistone. At length, a gate on the left announces arrival at Wogden Foot.

An information board tells how the site (once busy railway sidings) supports many species, including some uncommon in a gritstone area such as this.

Beyond Wogden Foot, a cutting ends, permitting views of rough pasture and open moor. The approach to Cote Bank Bridge is heralded by power lines crossing the trackbed. Within 100 yards, turn left through a gap in a wall. Follow an enclosed path parallel to the railway as far as the bridge. Double back left over a stile. An enclosed way (note the paving) descends towards the Upper Don on the valley floor. At the end, climb a stile and turn left. Almost immediately, cross the river on a footbridge. Turn right alongside a wall. Cross Town Brook, a tributary of the Upper Don, via a footbridge. Bear left up a green lane. On reaching Soughley, cross a stile. Keep left of a barn conversion and cottages. Turn left up a grassy way. Go through a gate into a field. Bear half-right up the field to its top-left corner.

Amid improving valley views, climb a ladder-stile. In the next field, bear half-left to a gate near the opposite corner. Go through the gate. Head slightly right to a wall corner. Turn right on a track on the edge of a wood. Climb a ladder-stile and follow the track sharp left. (The view into the valley is superb.) Pass through another gate. Bear right with the track. Take the

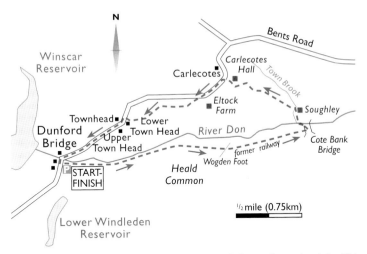

right-hand option at a fork. Keep climbing. Look for a stile on the right. This admits to a path enclosed by mossy walls. It rises through trees, keeping left of the tiny Parish Church of St Mary. Swing left through a gate, emerging on a minor road in the village of Carlecotes. Turn left. Follow the road towards Townhead, a hamlet.

Note on the right a former school house with an 1830 datestone.

Shortly after a caravan site, angle left down a stony track. When the track (now surfaced) dips to enter a farmyard, climb a stile on the right. Head along the bottom edge of a steeply sloping field, shadowing a wall.

A stile in the corner admits to an enclosed way. Bend left into another field. Maintain the earlier line over paving along its top edge, making for Townhead, with the wall now to the right. Cross a stile in the corner. Keep ahead along the bottom edge of a field. At the end, climb a stile to the left of a gate into another field. Within 50 yards, switch to the other side of the wall via a stile. Pause to look down the valley in the direction of Penistone. Follow the wall. Cross a stile and pass in front of a log cabin. Join a drive. Climb a stile to the right of a gate. Bend right, to emerge in Townhead on the minor road linking Carlecotes and Dunford Bridge. Turn left along the undulating road to Dunford Bridge. Cross the Upper Don, before turning into the car park.

On the descent to the car park, note up to the right the embankment of Winscar Reservoir and, across the valley, Lower Windleden Reservoir.

The upper Dearne Valley

Distance: 4 miles (6.5km). Time: 2-2½ hours.
Start/parking: Shelley, Kirklees Light Railway station (free parking), grid ref 208101.
Finish: Clayton West, Kirklees Light Railway station; grid ref 257112.
Terrain: gentle – field paths, tracks and roads. Height gained: 260 feet (80m).
Refreshments/facilities: cafés and toilets at Shelley and Clayton West stations.
Public transport: Buses 80 & 81 (Huddersfield–Clayton West), Bus 82
(Huddersfield–Denby Dale), Buses 435 & 436 (Wakefield–Holmfirth).
Map: Ordnance Survey Explorer 288 Bradford & Huddersfield.

*Let the train take some of the strain on this lovely linear walk shadowing the
narrow-gauge Kirklees Light Railway (www.kirkleeslightrailway.com,
telephone 01484 865727). Park at Clayton West station and board a steam
train to Shelley, then walk back through the peaceful upper Dearne Valley.*

Leave Shelley station via a gate on the right admitting to a track. Pass
through another gate (if it is locked or you cannot negotiate a gap on the
right, ask station staff to open it). Turn left beneath twin railway bridges
over a minor road. Within 100 yards, turn left over a stile. Walk along the
left edge of a field. Cross a stile and keep forward on a track over a standard-
gauge railway. The lane peters out at a stable. Bear half-left over a stile. Hug
the left edge of fields to cross another stile. Pass to the left of farm buildings.
Climb a stile and follow the farm's drive to a minor road.

With the Kirklees Light Railway (KLR) on an embankment up to the left,
cross the road and follow an enclosed path. On joining a track, continue
forward. Emerge on a minor road near Shelley Woodhouse, a hamlet
dominated by the 1,084-foot (330m) Emley Moor transmitter. Turn right.
Within 50 yards, bear left along an enclosed way. Pass a pond which helped
power a textile mill (now flats) on the left. Drop to another minor road.
Cross, turn right and enter Skelmanthorpe. Opposite the higher entrance to
Shelley College, turn left over a stile and down the left edge of a field.

Cross a stile in the bottom corner of the field. Join an enclosed path. This
bends right before descending steps and crossing the KLR on a footbridge
close to the eastern portal of Shelley Woodhouse Tunnel. Rise to the right
from the footbridge. Keep forward over a stile and down the right edge of a
field. Pass through a gate. Cross a stile in the field corner. Negotiate an
enclosed section to arrive at an unsurfaced lane. Go over a cattle grid

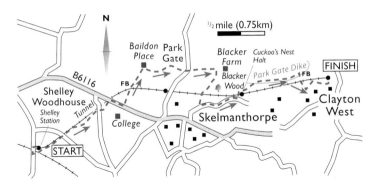

opposite. Follow an unsurfaced lane across Baildon Dike. Just before the buildings of Baildon Place, bear right over a stile. Follow a track beneath what appear to be grassed-over spoil heaps. The track, with Baildon Dike to the right, becomes enclosed. Climb a stile. Continue through trees to emerge on a minor road in the hamlet of Park Gate. Turn left.

Where the road begins climbing steeply, bear right along a lane. As you approach Blacker Farm, turn right over a stile and down the left edge of a field. Cross a stile in the corner to enter Blacker Wood. The path bends right. Cross Park Gate Dike on a footbridge. Climb to a stile on the right taking you out of the wood. Walk up the left edge of a field. On encountering a stile on the left, bear half-right and pass beneath a bridge carrying the KLR.

An enclosed way rises to unsurfaced Pilling Lane. Turn left, soon leaving the houses behind. Follow this track some distance through a surprisingly secluded landscape. Soon after the track begins to rise, take another track on the left. This drops to pass beneath the KLR by the unused Cuckoo's Nest Halt, terminus of the line in its early years. At a gate, climb a stile on the right. Angle half-left across the top of a sloping field, passing between wooden stockades protecting young trees. Through a wall gap, maintain the line to cross a stile in the bottom corner of another sloping field. Bear right on a track alongside Park Gate Dike.

With the track becoming increasingly obvious, shadow the stream through fields. It becomes enclosed by trees and arrives at a fork. Bear left. Where the trees on the right end, turn right up an enclosed path to pass beneath the KLR. Climb a stile and cross a field, making for another stile ahead. Cross a stream via a footbridge. Enter a way between houses in Clayton West. Turn left on the A636. Within 200 yards, turn right up Park Mill Way. Follow it to the left through an industrial estate built on the site of Park Mill Colliery, to return to Clayton West station car park.

11

The reservoirs of Holme

Distance: 4 miles (6.5km). Time: 2-2½ hours.
Start/finish: Meal Mill Road, Holme, free street parking; grid ref 057109.
(Alternative start/finish: Digley Reservoir, free car park, grid ref 070112;
Ramsden Reservoir, free car park, grid ref 054116.)
Terrain: Several undemanding ups and downs – field paths, steps,
tracks and roads. Height gained: 835 feet (255m).
Refreshments/facilities: pubs in Holme and Holmbridge; toilets in Holme.
Public transport: Bus 314 (Huddersfield–Holme), Bus 951
(Huddersfield–Glossop), Bus H7 (Holmfirth–Holmbridge Circular).
Map: Ordnance Survey Explorer OL1 Peak District (Dark Peak).

Glorious scenery and views ignite this varied circuit from Holme, a hamlet near the head of the Holme Valley, close to the Peak District National Park boundary. The route encounters four impressive reservoirs, numerous streams and a delightful waterfall.

Walk up Meal Mill Road from Woodhead Road in Holme. Shortly after a play area, bear right along an enclosed way. A stile admits to a field. Angle half-right and negotiate a stile in its corner.

To the right, the Holme Valley stretches away to Holmfirth, with Emley Moor transmitter on the skyline. Ahead, Digley Reservoir soon joins the scene.

Cross a field bottom and go through a stile. The obvious path bends left. Shadowing a field boundary, pass through two gap-stiles and a step-stile. Bear half-right to a stile. Maintain the line in the next field, climbing a stile. Drop to a path round the reservoir. Turn left and go through a gate. Head to the far side of the adjacent wall via a gate. Descend through trees and heather. Use steps to reach the dam separating Digley and Bilberry reservoirs.

There was a catastrophic flood on 5th February 1852 when Bilberry Reservoir burst its banks. A stream had not been diverted properly twelve years earlier when the reservoir was built. Gradual weakening ensued until, following a fortnight of storms, a torrent poured down the valley into Holmbridge and Holmfirth. Eighty-one died, and four textile mills were among numerous buildings either damaged or destroyed.

Cross the dam. Turn left up a track. Pass through a gate and double back on

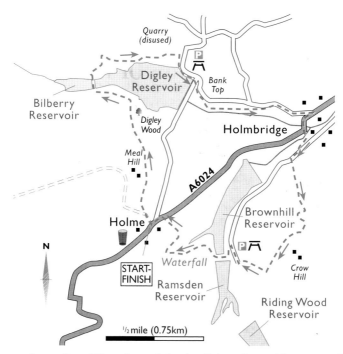

a rougher surface. Where the track levels off, keep forward between walls. In mixed woodland, the track descends and bends right. Keep left with a fence and over a stream before climbing steps. Pass through a gap and drop to an enclosed track. Bear left. The route rises to emerge from trees, then descends towards Digley Reservoir's free car park in a former quarry.

Digley Reservoir was constructed in 1954 on the site of two mills in the path of the 1852 flood. Its car park is an alternative start-finish point for the walk.

Keep ahead to a gate. Turn right on a minor road. Pass a kissing-gate on the right leading to a picnic area. The head of the Holme Valley and Holme Moss transmitter are well seen. Do not cross the dam, but continue downhill. Look for a kissing-gate on the right as the road curves left, and go through the gate. Bear left with a wall. Descend steps into a wood above the River Holme. Angle half-left and drop to a stile in a corner. Descend steps to a lane. Turn left. With the river below, follow the lane past a tiny cricket ground to the A6024 in Holmbridge.

Turn right, passing St David's Church. Cross the River Holme. At a sign for

The heron is a distinctive sight near any stretch of water.

Ramsden Reservoir, bear left on Bank Lane. Follow the lane, right, climbing steeply. Then, 25 yards after a junction with Dobb Top Road, turn left by a finger-post along a lane. In a square, keep forward. Pass through a kissing-gate to the right of an end-terrace cottage. Cross the cottage yard and go through a kissing-gate. Maintain the same line, keeping left of huts and a stream, and bear slightly left. Go through a gate into a tree-lined ravine.

Climb steadily, ignoring a stile on the left. Continue forward, with the stream down to the right. As the ravine becomes shallower, go through a wall gap. Bear right over the stream. Climb a bank, before swinging left up the other side of the watercourse. At the top of the ravine, bend right and make for a stile leading to a green lane.

Pause to admire a fine view encompassing Castle Hill, Brownhill and Digley reservoirs, Holme and the head of the Holme Valley.

Turn right, sticking with a wall on the right. When the wall ends, angle half-right down a pasture to a stile. Bear right at a fork. Descend an enclosed way on the edge of a wood. Cross a stream. Bend left to come out via a stile on a minor road above Ramsden Reservoir.

Ramsden Reservoir has free parking and picnic tables, on the left. The parking area is also an alternative start-finish point for the walk.

Turn right. Within 100 yards, double back on a track. Turn right, along the dam separating Ramsden and Brownhill reservoirs. Swing right and climb left through trees. The path levels off before dropping to a footbridge over a stream. Note the pretty waterfall. Cross, double back and rise to a stile. Leaving the trees, bear half-left across a field to twin stiles admitting to an enclosed way. Move to the far side of a wall via a gate on the left. Go through a gate by an unusual subterranean house with a turf roof. Keep forward to the A6024. Turn left, passing a former school with a 1694 datestone, and the start point is 100 yards on the right.

Around Netherthong

Distance: 5 miles (8km). Time: 2½-3 hours.
Start/parking: Towngate, Netherthong, free street parking; grid ref 139098.
Terrain: fairly gentle, some climbing. Height gained: 625 feet (190m).
Refreshments/facilities: pubs and shop in Netherthong; no public toilets.
Public transport: Bus 308 (Huddersfield–Holmfirth), Bus 335
(Slaithwaite–Meltham–Holmfirth), Bus H5 (Holmfirth Circular).
Map: Ordnance Survey Explorer 288 Bradford & Huddersfield.

Little exertion is required to enjoy stunning views on a pleasant circuit from the hilltop village of Netherthong. The route visits Oldfield, a neighbouring hamlet, and includes a charming stretch in Honley Woods. Much is on a breezy plateau from which a sizeable chunk of western Kirklees is visible.

Start from Towngate, by All Saints' Church, in the constricted centre of Netherthong. (Buses stop here and the village shop is opposite.) Walk downhill a few paces. When Towngate drops to the right, keep ahead on Church Street. Continue into School Street, passing the Clothiers Arms. Immediately after the village primary school, descend steeply left on a cobbled path. Cross a road at its foot. Climb a lane opposite, bending right and left. Pass the Cricketers Arms. Keep ahead in the direction indicated by a fingerpost. Go through a gate next to a cider maker's and enter a field. Keep to the field's right edge. Within 25 yards, bear left at a fork. A clear path angles half-left up the field. Pass through a gap, then maintain the same direction in the next.

Pause to absorb a superb view encompassing Netherthong (on a lofty ridge), the 1,084-foot (330m) Emley Moor transmitter, Castle Hill (topped by Victoria Tower) and the Ainley Top watershed, separating Huddersfield and Halifax. Castle Hill is the site of an Iron Age fort; its inhabitants would have no trouble recognising this classic South Pennines scene.

Shadow a wall on the left. Go through a gap and follow an enclosed way to a track in the hamlet of Oldfield. Turn right and follow the track, soon surfaced, between houses to Oldfield Road.

Note the former school and its 1838 datestone.

Cross the road and head along an enclosed path almost opposite.

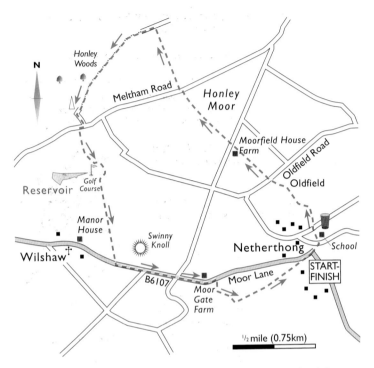

The view from this plateau is sublime, with Honley down to the right.

Descend gently to the drive of Moorfield House Farm. Emerge on Bradshaw Road. Cross and follow a grassy track alongside cottages. A gap admits to a fenced path through a field. The fences are left behind at a stile. Keep to the right edge of several fields. Arrive at Meltham Road. Turn left for 100 yards before bearing right by a fingerpost on a walled track. Passing a farm, the track leads unerringly to Hassocks Lane. Turn left on the lane.

Hassocks Lane hugs the top edge of Honley Woods. Note the colourful 'welcome' sign created in metal by local artist Cate Clark.

The lane soon becomes a path as it heads through the trees. (Don't be tempted by paths bearing off right deeper into the wood on this delightful section.) When the path emerges on a lane by a telecoms mast, turn left to rejoin Meltham Road. With the distinctive profile of West Nab ahead, bear right for 25 yards. Then turn left by a fingerpost over a stile. Keep forward across a field to locate a stile, partly obscured by holly bushes, in its far boundary. Follow the left edge of the next field.

The 750-foot (228m) Holme Moss transmitter dominates the skyline.

Pass through a gate. Drop half-left to the corner of a field. Climb a stile on the left, entering a wood. Within 25 yards, turn right on a stony track. Initially, this walled way descends steeply. It swings right and levels off, passing Meltham golf course, before bending left and climbing steadily.

The small town of Meltham, backed by West Nab and Meltham Cop, is now visible over to your right.

At length, the track acquires a concrete surface and meets the B6107 between Netherthong and Wilshaw.

The domed summit on the left is Swinny Knoll.

Turn left and follow this lightly trafficked road mostly downhill for about half a mile (0.8km) to Moor Gate Farm. Just beyond the buildings, climb steps in a hedge on the right. A fingerpost aids navigation. Rise up the left edge of a field. Two-thirds of the way along the adjacent wall, cross a stile. Angle half-left to the opposite corner of the neighbouring field.

The reed bunting may be seen on farmland and in damp areas.

Emerge via a stile on a walled lane. Turn right. Just before a gate, bear left over a stile into a field.

Netherthong is now below. To the right, a swathe of the Holme Valley can be seen, with Holmfirth and Thongsbridge prominent. The Emley Moor transmitter, Castle Hill, Victoria Tower and the moors above Halifax complete a breathtaking panorama.

An obvious path trends half-right to a wall, which it shadows before drifting half-left to a stile. Cross a field beyond. Go through a gate admitting to an enclosed way. This bends left between gardens to emerge via a drive by houses. Bear right to West End in Netherthong. The church is 150 yards down to the right.

Hepworth and district

Distance: 5 miles (8km). Time: 2½-3 hours.
Start/parking: Towngate, Hepworth, free street parking; grid ref 162066.
Terrain: steep ascents and descents – field paths, steps, tracks and roads.
Height gained: 870 feet (265m).
Refreshments/facilities: pub in Hepworth; garden centre cafés in Totties.
Public transport: Buses 313 & X13 (Huddersfield–Hepworth).
Map: Ordnance Survey Explorer 288 Bradford & Huddersfield.

Hepworth, a tiny village of narrow streets and small cottages, is set amid typically wild Pennine scenery. This remarkably varied circuit, all ups and downs, explores the beautiful landscape surrounding Hepworth and provides numerous outstanding views.

From Towngate in Hepworth, keep right of the Butchers Arms and descend to a junction with Butt Lane. Bear left and drop into a narrow valley. Follow the road round a sharp bend. Go through a gate by a fingerpost on the left. Follow an undulating path through Morton Wood.

This is a classic Pennine clough, along whose floor flows a lively stream.

Cross the watercourse several times on boulders and footbridges. The path bears right and shadows another stream. Keep left of a ruin. Emerge via steps on a track in the hamlet of Upper House. Bear left.

Follow the rising track between cottages to a junction with a minor road. Turn left for 100 yards. Then leave the road via a stile on the right. Ascend the right edge of a field. Keep right of a house called Springhead and join a track. (Bowshaw Whams Reservoir is over to the left.) Turn right on Scholes Moor Road, descending steadily.

The panorama ahead is breathtaking. After the clammy confines of the clough, the feeling of light, air and space is wonderful. Hepworth is picked out by the spire of Holy Trinity Church. Obvious landmarks are the 1,084-foot (330m) Emley Moor transmitter and Victoria Tower atop Castle Hill.

Within 50 yards of passing the oddly named Little Cake (a minor road), leave Scholes Moor Road by a wall gap on the left. A fingerpost marks the spot. With the village of Scholes down to the right, keep forward along the

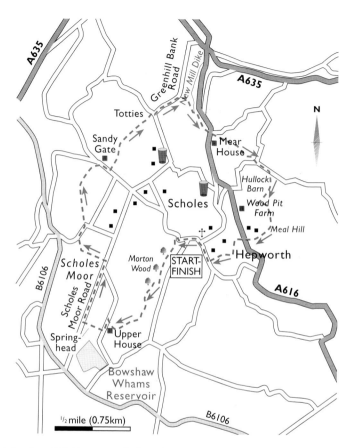

left edge of fields to a walled track. Go through a gap opposite. Drop half-right with a wall to a minor road. Climb to a sharp bend by a farm. Bear left at a fingerpost on a walled track.

There are splendid views into the Holme Valley. Holmfirth is far below, whilst the Holme Moss transmitter guards the dale head.

The track ends at Sandy Gate, a minor road. Turn right for 150 yards to a green. Bear left on Sike Lane, a walled track. It descends to become surfaced in the hamlet of Totties (meaning 'top of the hill'). Turn right, then keep left of a tiny green, passing seventeenth-century cottages. Descend on Greenhill Bank Road.

Totties is home to two well-signposted garden centres, where refreshments can be obtained.

When the road swings left, leave it via a path on the right by a fingerpost. Drop through trees. Keep forward to emerge in a modern housing development, part of which was Wildspur Mills. Continue ahead between multi-storey houses and bear left. Do not climb left to the A616, but turn right in front of traditional terraced cottages. Keep forward on a wooded path shoehorned between a private drive and New Mill Dike. The mill dam is above the stream. Bear left at a fork. Climb steeply through trees to the A616 at Mear House.

Cross to Butterley Lane. After a few paces, bear right by a fingerpost. Climb steps and follow an enclosed way right and left between houses. Rise to a stile and enter a field. Maintain the same direction up its left edge.

As you climb, the views open out. The hamlet clinging to the hillside opposite is Jackson Bridge.

Cross a stile into another field. Bear half-right. Crest a rise and make for a stile to the left of a gate. In the next field, aim half-right to a gate admitting to the yard of Meltham House Farm. Walk across the front of the house and leave via a gate on the right.

With Hepworth on the far side of this narrow valley, turn left up a minor road as far as a fingerpost on the right. A path drops through trees and above Hullock Barn. Descend steps and keep left of this barn conversion. Go down a grassy bank and over a stile into a pasture. Keep forward on a path which bends half-left to a stile in a corner. With Wood Pit Farm below, turn right along the top of the adjacent field. At the far side, bear left down its right edge to cross a stile in the bottom corner. Follow a partially stepped path through trees. Cross a stream and emerge on a minor road.

Turn left and climb steadily. Bear right by a fingerpost through a gateway when the road bends up to the left. Join a track, which becomes surfaced after the hamlet of Meal Hill. Descend to the A616. Cross and follow an enclosed way opposite. Drop through a wood to a broader path. Turn left for 100 yards. Cross a stream via a footbridge on the right. With Hepworth above, climb the right edge of a field. A stile admits to the adjacent field. Ascend the field's left edge to emerge via steps on Towngate.

The upper Holme Valley

Distance: 5 miles (8km). Time: 2½-3 hours.
Start/parking: Holmfirth bus station, pay & display car parks in Holmfirth; grid ref 141082.
Terrain: steep ascents and descents. Height gained: 890 feet (270m).
Refreshments/facilities: pubs, shops and eateries in Holmfirth; pubs in Holmbridge and Upperthong; toilets opposite Holmfirth bus station.
Public transport: Buses 308, 312, 313, 314 & 316 (Huddersfield–Holmfirth), Buses 435 & 436 (Wakefield–Holmfirth), Bus 951 (Huddersfield–Glossop).
Map: Ordnance Survey Explorer 288 Bradford & Huddersfield.

Ups and downs abound on this delightful walk which displays the upper Holme Valley to advantage. The effort is rewarded with fine views. A varied route includes a stretch alongside the Holme, and visits the villages of Holmbridge and Upperthong.

From the bus station, walk alongside the Holme, bearing right into Victoria Street. At traffic lights, turn left on the A6024. Follow it to the second fingerpost on the left by the Toad & Tatie pub. Join access to a housing development. Keep ahead on an initially cobbled way.

The adjacent Holme looks benign, but flooded disastrously in 1777, 1852 and 1944.

Track a path along its wooded bank. At a junction of ways near a mill chimney, stick with the river. Ignoring a footbridge, pass the mill's dam and shadow its race. Shortly before another old mill, cross the Holme on a footbridge. Follow the path left. Bear right through a kissing-gate. Ascend a field. Shortly, bear half-right to climb a stile in a corner. Turn left. Rise more steeply alongside a clough to emerge on Acre Lane via a stile opposite Hill Cottage. Turn right and drop to Dobb.

The view across the fields of Water Side to the far side of the dale is superb. The side-valley (source of the Holme) housing Digley and Bilberry reservoirs is also visible, whilst the Holme Moss transmitter crowns the high ground ahead.

At a T-junction in Dobb, by Hollin Brigg House, cross a minor road. Bear down to the right through a wall gap by a fingerpost. Cross Dobb Dike on a

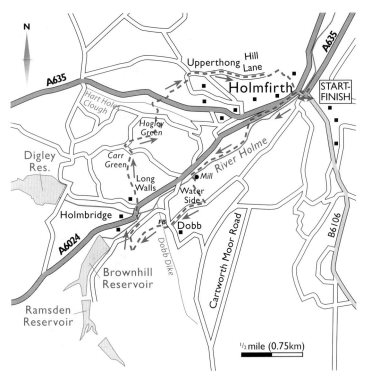

footbridge. Go up a field to steps. Amid trees, turn right. Continue on through a gate into a field. Keep ahead along the bottom edge of several fields to a farm. Climb a stile. Cross a track to another stile. This admits to a sunken way angling up a field edge to a stile in its corner.

Now in a wooded clough, turn right. Shadow a stream through a gate. Keep right of huts. Emerge, via two gates and the yard of Kiln House Clough Farm, in a square of dwellings.

Note that the lintel stone of 21a is inscribed IWI and 1910.

Keep ahead on a track to a T-junction with a minor road. Turn right. Descend into Holmbridge. Bear right on the A6024 to cross the Holme. Pass St David's Church and the village's engagingly bijou cricket ground.

Swing right with the A6024. By the Bridge Tavern, turn sharp left along Field End Lane. Within 25 yards, bear right by a fingerpost up steps. Follow an enclosed way past houses. Cross a road and continue between red-brick semis opposite to emerge in a field. Ascend the near edge of this field and several more on a clear path.

The view up and down the Holme Valley improves as height is gained. Much of the earlier route can be traced.

As the path levels, funnel between walls and over a stile ahead. Drop down field edges, through a gate. Go along an enclosed way to a minor road. Turn left. Rise to a fork in front of cottages at Carr Green. Now on the level, turn right. Within 100 yards, bear half-right opposite Garden Field Cottage along a track.

Enter a field via a stile. Follow a clear path shadowing the boundaries of several fields. Climb a final stile to emerge amid a group of dwellings known as Hogley Green. Follow its gravel access to the left. On reaching a

The hazel: leaf, catkins and nuts.

minor road, turn right. Bear left at a fork. Descend into Hart Holes Clough. Cross a stream in sylvan surroundings. Follow the lane up to the A635. Cross the road. Ascend an enclosed track to Upperthong.

Turn left on a minor road (Broad Lane). Reach the summit of the walk at a bend. Bear right along Thong Town Gate. Pass a traditional phone box now used as a book and video exchange, the Royal Oak pub and a multi-storeyed former handloom weavers' cottage to reach a junction of ways. Keep ahead on Hill Lane.

Initially surfaced, this becomes a classic green lane offering wonderful views encompassing Castle Hill, adorned by Victoria Tower, and the Emley Moor transmitter.

Hill Lane becomes surfaced again at Hill. Descend to a fingerpost. This directs you to an enclosed way keeping to the right of a house, Ashleigh. Drop steeply on steps to Holt Lane. Turn right and immediately left down Cooper Lane. Opposite Oakfield, bear right by a fingerpost on an enclosed path which comes out in a park. Bear right over cobbles. Descend past a play area to the A6024. Turn left to the traffic lights in the centre of Holmfirth. Bear right on Victoria Street to return to the bus station.

The delights of Denby Dale

Distance: 5 miles (8km). Time: 2½-3 hours.
Start/parking: Denby Dale Bus/Rail Interchange, free street parking on
Station Lane in Denby Dale; grid ref 223084.
Terrain: very limited climbing. Height gained: 570 feet (175m).
Refreshments/facilities: pubs and shops in Denby Dale and Upper
Cumberworth; pubs in Upper Denby and Lower Denby.
Public transport: Bus 24 (Barnsley–Denby Dale), Buses 82, 83, 84
(Huddersfield–Denby Dale); train (Huddersfield–Penistone–Sheffield line).
Map: Ordnance Survey Explorer OL1 Peak District (Dark Peak).

The Industrial Revolution spawned Denby Dale, which remains a working village famous for enormous pies and a towering railway viaduct. This charming circuit explores the wonderfully varied countryside around Denby Dale, and visits the neighbouring communities of Upper Cumberworth, Upper Denby and Lower Denby.

Walk up Station Lane, passing the bus turning circle, and follow an enclosed way to the right of the station. Cross the railway. Continue past a quarry to climb a stile. Turn sharp left along the edge of a field. In the corner, bear right and track the field boundary.

Look back to view Denby Dale Viaduct, opened in 1880. Its twenty-one arches replaced a flimsy wooden structure.

Near the far end of the field, drift right to a stile in a corner. This admits to a fenced path. Approaching a minor road, swing left and cross a stile into a field. Bear half-right to another stile. Emerge on a minor road. Cross, climb a stile and follow the left edge of a field.

The 1,084-foot (330m) Emley Moor transmitter is on the right.

Bear half-left on reaching a wall corner, aiming for a stile between red-brick bungalows (a tree marks the spot) on the far side of the field. An enclosed way emerges on a minor road in Upper Cumberworth.

Turn left. Continue to a junction with the A635. (The Star pub is opposite and a post office/shop on the right.) Cross and follow Carr Hill Road. Where it bends right, bear left on Park Lane. This becomes a stony track. Follow it

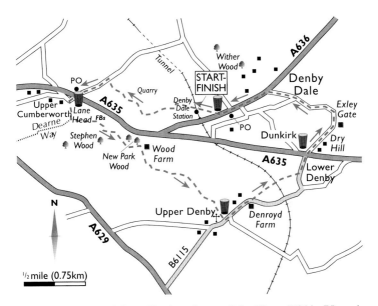

right and left through Lane Head, a cluster of dwellings. Within 75 yards, when the track swings right, climb a stile on the left. Bear half-left along a field edge. A stile admits to Stephen Wood. The key is to follow Dearne Way indicators. Bear left at an immediate fork.

The adjacent spring provided Upper Cumberworth's drinking water until 1895.

Drop through trees. Pass the spring's confluence with the infant River Dearne. Bear right at a fork. At the next fork, bear right. Climb a stile to emerge at a junction of tracks above a waterfall. Cross the Dearne via a footbridge. Go through a gate and continue along a broad track amid trees. Bear left at the next two forks. Cross a stream and climb a stile. Ignore a stile ahead, instead bearing right on a fenced track. Shortly, turn right, cross a footbridge over the Dearne and ascend steps. Climb a stile. Bear half-left across a field to a stile accessing New Park Wood. Angle half-right and rise to a grassy track. Turn left. Reach, via a kissing-gate, a lane by Wood Farm.

Turn right. With the farm to your left, continue to a right bend. Keep forward on a more overgrown surface. At a point where this byway bends right to a gate, drop left over a stile. Descend to a stream crossing. Follow a wall half-left and right to emerge via a stile on a stony track. Turn left. Climb a stile next to a gate. Follow the walled track to another stile/gate combination. In the field beyond, keep forward alongside a wall on the left. Climb a stile in the corner. Bear right along the edge of a field. At a fork in its corner, ignore an option left, and pass through a gate. Bear half-right up the edge of a steep field. Go through a gap. Maintain the line across the left edge of several fields and a 50-yard stretch of walled lane. Skirt the boundary of a cricket ground. Emerge on a minor road in Upper Denby.

Turn left through the village, passing the George pub. On reaching dwellings near Denroyd Farm, bear left by a footpath sign over a stile.

Absorb a superb view in following the right edge of two fields separated by a gateway. In the bottom corner of the second, bear left 15 yards to cross a stile. Drop through a field. Go over the railway.

The green woodpecker can be identified by its dark green upperparts, paler green belly and bright red cap.

Bear left to the corner of the next field, then right along its left edge. Near a cottage, kink left through a gap. Follow the right edge of a field to emerge via a gate on a minor road in Lower Denby.

Turn left. By the Dunkirk Inn, cross the A635. Continue past Dry Hill, a hamlet. On reaching Exley Gate (a collection of cottages), turn left on a minor road signed for Denby Dale. Stick with the road when it bends left and descend steadily. After a level stretch, where the road begins to climb, bear right down a track through trees. This narrows into a sunken path. Cross the Dearne on a footbridge. Bear left on a lane to a minor road. Turn right and rise to the A636. Turn left, passing through Denby Dale. With the viaduct ahead, 50 yards after Wesley Terrace, bear right on a surfaced lane. When it swings left, keep forward on a tarmac path and climb to Station Lane.

Discovering the Colne Valley

> **Distance: 5½ miles (9km). Time: 2½-3 hours.**
> **Start/parking: Marsden railway station, free street parking; grid ref 046118.**
> **Terrain: some short ascents and descents. Height gained: 575 feet (175m).**
> **Refreshments/facilities: shops, pubs and toilets in Marsden and Slaithwaite.**
> **Public transport: Buses 182, 183, 184, 185, 186 (Huddersfield–Marsden);**
> **train (Huddersfield-Stalybridge-Manchester line).**
> **Map: Ordnance Survey Explorer OL21 South Pennines.**

The Colne Valley communities of Marsden and Slaithwaite (pronounced Sla'wit) grew with the Industrial Revolution, and former textile mills still dominate. The two communities are linked by the trans-Pennine Huddersfield Narrow Canal, whose towpath is followed on the outward section before a high-level return to Marsden along the dale's southern flank.

From the station, join the adjacent Huddersfield Narrow Canal towpath at lock 42E (E for East) opposite the Railway pub. Go under bridge 59 and follow the towpath for almost three miles (5km). During the walk's early stages, locks come thick and fast.

Opened in 1811, the 20-mile (32km) canal made a key contribution to the valley before inexorable decline resulted in its abandonment in 1944. From 1974, Huddersfield Canal Society volunteers began restoration and the canal reopened to full navigation in 2001. Marsden Flight illustrates how much height had to be gained to breach the Pennine watershed using the 3-mile (5km) Standedge Tunnel, Britain's longest, highest and deepest canal bore. Note the basins (or pounds) in which boats could load and unload or moor whilst waiting to enter locks.

The River Colne flows alongside by lock 35E. Sparth Reservoir, one of ten built to supply the canal, is reached at lock 33E. A more open stretch ensues before the canal passes between derelict Cellars Clough Mill and Sandhill Cottages, built in 1860.

Above lock 31E, Booth winding hole is encountered. The former lock-keeper's cottage dates from 1858.

The meandering River Colne rejoins at locks 30E and 26E. After bridge 48, trees overhang the canal and ferns fringe its banks. The guillotine tail-gate

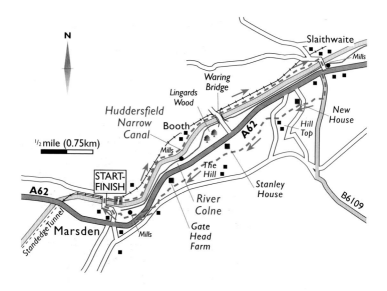

at lock 24E — unique on a narrow canal — heralds Slaithwaite. Alongside Upper Mills, the towpath broadens and passes the Moonraker, a floating café.

Restoring the canal through the village required serious engineering. Note the former Slaithwaite Free School, built in 1721, on the left.

Leave the canal at bridge 44 and turn right along Britannia Road.

To visit Slaithwaite, keep ahead on Carr Lane.

When Britannia Road bends left, bear right up Ned Lane. Cross the A62 and ascend Varley Road, the B6109. With Kitchen Clough down to the left, continue to the last dwelling (Mansergh House) on the right. A stile admits to a sunken way. This bends right and left into a field. Keep forward to a stile.

Look back for a superb view of Slaithwaite, dominated by railway viaducts and mills. The constricted nature of the Colne Valley is obvious from here.

Follow a path along field edges to a minor road in New House. Turn right to another minor road. Cross and keep forward on a lane between houses. By a fingerpost, take a track on the left. Continue past cottages to climb a stile into a field. Negotiate another stile and enter a broadening field.

Marsden, sheltered by a bleak bowl of moorland, is visible ahead.

Stick to the right edge of the field and climb a stile in its corner. Maintain the line along the top edge of the next field. After a stile, bear half-right beside a garden. Emerge via a stile on a minor road in Hill Top. Turn right. Within 25 yards, bear left by a fingerpost along Hollins Lane. Follow this track to its terminus at Old Hollins.

Keep left of farm buildings and climb a stile. Continue along the top edge of a field. Cross a stream and the bottom edge of a field to a derelict house, a forlorn spectacle. Follow an enclosed way. When this bends right, enter a field via a stile on the left. Shadow its bottom edge before rising half-left. Pass to the right of a wall corner. Cross a marshy area to a stile.

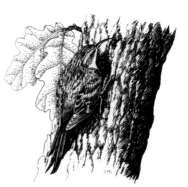

An unobtrusive bird, the treecreeper may be spotted circling up a tree in its search for insects.

Walk along the top edge of the field beyond. By a telegraph post, bear half-left up an enclosed way below the Hill (a farm). Climb a stile and turn right down another enclosed way. Within 25 yards, a stile admits to a field. Track its bottom edge. Maintain the line over a stream, with a waterfall hidden in a wooded clough. A kissing-gate admits to a plantation. Beyond this, a junction of tracks is reached by engraved stone memorial seats. Climb a stile in a wall corner. Bear slightly left across pasture. Climb a stile by a gate. Continue along the bottom edge of another pasture, passing through a gap between walls. Reach a gate via the top edge of a field. Join a green lane. On reaching houses, this becomes surfaced and acquires the name Gate Head.

Descend to Stubbin Road. Bear left. Turn right on the B6107. Drop to the A62. Cross and head along Brougham Road, passing the vast Crowther Bruce's New Mills, to arrive at the Mechanics Hall in the heart of Marsden.

Built in 1861, the Mechanics Hall houses a tourist information centre and is an arts hub.

A lofty circuit of Meltham

Distance: 6 miles (10km). Time: 3-3½ hours.
Start/parking: Meltham bus turning circle on Parkin Lane, free parking in
Carlisle Street and Clark Lane car parks; grid ref 100105.
Terrain: undemanding ascents and descents – field paths, tracks and roads.
Height gained: 700 feet (215m).
Refreshments/facilities: eateries, shops, pubs and toilets in Meltham.
Public transport: Buses 321 & 324 (Huddersfield–Meltham), Bus 335
(Holmfirth–Pole Moor), Bus 388 (Huddersfield Royal Infirmary–Meltham),
Bus 911 (Meltham–Farnley Tyas Circular), Bus 933 (Meltham Circular).
Map: Ordnance Survey Explorer 288 Bradford & Huddersfield.

Every aspect of Meltham is seen from a route encircling this attractive little
town. It passes beneath the hills of West Nab and Meltham Cop, and crosses
the dam of the loftily located Blackmoorfoot Reservoir. A sizeable chunk
makes use of elevated paths shadowing the reservoir's catchwater drains.
The views throughout are superb.

Start from the bus turning circle on Parkin Lane, close to Meltham centre.
Walk a few paces to the junction with Holmfirth Road (B6107) and turn left.

Pass the impressive Odd Fellows Hall, built in 1851.

Leave Holmfirth Road via Tinker Lane on the right. Where it bends right,
bear left along an enclosed way. Cross a minor road and skirt allotments. A
kissing-gate admits to a lane. Turn right. Soon unsurfaced, the lane rises
steadily and offers improving views down to the left into Royd Edge
Clough. Turn right on joining another track. This soon swings left and starts
to descend.

A glorious panorama to the right encompasses Meltham Cop, Meltham (at
the head of a tributary valley), Castle Hill and the Emley Moor transmitter.

Cross a catchwater drain. Climb a stile to join its right bank. Follow a clear
path, interrupted only by numerous substantial stone bridges over the drain.

The drain contains variable amounts of water and vegetation, and has the
appearance of a mini-canal. Where the banks are free of trees, the views
over Meltham and down the valley towards Huddersfield are breathtaking.

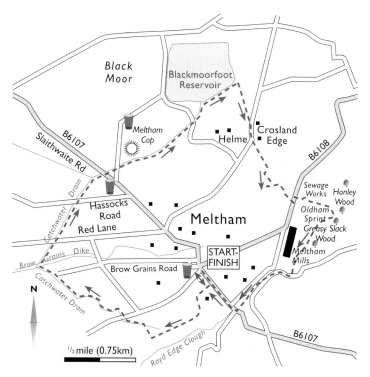

At length, soon after crossing Brow Grains Road, another catchwater drain is reached.

The stream tumbling off the moor is Brow Grains Dike.

Cross lock-type gates which control water movement. Bear right along this second channel. It is wider and contains more water. Several bridges, masterpieces of Victorian engineering, are encountered. Cross Red Lane, Hassocks Road, Slaithwaite Road and the Meltham to Blackmoorfoot road, keeping faith with the drain's right bank. Pass beneath the delightful dome of Meltham Cop. Continue above Helme, a hamlet. Shortly after crossing the Helme to Blackmoorfoot road, the path reaches the dam of Blackmoorfoot Reservoir, hidden until the last moment. Turn right along the dam.

A vast sheet of water stretches away to the left, with the Colne Valley communities of Golcar and Scapegoat Hill on the horizon.

On reaching a minor road, turn right. It marks the start of a long descent to the valley floor. When the road expires amid a cluster of dwellings, keep forward on a sandy path.

This path offers a wonderful perspective of the distinctively profiled West Nab, in whose lee Meltham shelters.

Bear right on a minor road (Harrison Lane). Drop through Crosland Edge, a hamlet. When the road drops to the right at Two Hoots Barn, keep forward on a narrower way. Follow this between houses until it reaches Lower Edge Farm. Bear right at two forks in quick succession. Bend right to a house with a 1648 datestone above its lintel. Keep ahead through a gap admitting to a field. Ignoring the gate in front of you, turn sharp left along the field boundary. Climb a stile in the field corner. Descend to the right, arriving at the drive of a house called High Brow.

Turn left up this drive for a short distance. Bear right over a stile next to a gate. Follow a track (a shelf on the wooded hillside) round to the left. With a sewage works in sight on the valley floor, turn right over a fence (this is easily missed). Follow a path dropping steeply through trees. Keep left. Squeeze between a wall and holly bushes, with a stream below on the right. Emerge on a track opposite a bridge.

Until 1965 this bridge carried the Lockwood–Meltham branch railway.

Pass beneath the bridge. Cross a field to emerge on Huddersfield Road. Turn left. Within 100 yards, bear right by a fingerpost on a grassy track. Cross Hall Dike. Follow a fenced path left and right past the sewage works. On joining a minor road, bear left. When it peters out at the entrance to Bent Ley industrial estate, keep ahead on a tarmac lane. Within 25 yards (a waymark post is a handy guide), bear right into Honley Woods.

Local artist Cate Clark produced the colourful Honley Woods signs.

With Oldham Springs (a stream) on the right, follow a clear path rising through trees. At a T-junction, denoted by a White Rose Forest waymark post, turn right. This mostly level path merges with another track and leads unerringly past Meltham Mills to a minor road, Knowle Lane.

Turn right. Descend to a junction, briefly bearing left on Acre Lane. Leave it via steps on the right accessing a wood. Angle left on a clear path, shadowing a stream boasting a fine weir. Ignore a footbridge. Continue to the B6107. Turn right and follow it into Meltham. Parkin Lane soon appears on the right.